NO AR

essential careers™

CAREERS IN LANDSCAPING AND GARDENING

LARRY GERBER

ROSEN PUBLISHING®

NEW YORK

Published in 2014 by The Rosen Publishing Group, Inc.
29 East 21st Street, New York, NY 10010

Library of Congress Cataloging-in-Publication Data

Gerber, Larry, 1946–
Careers in landscaping and gardening/Larry Gerber.—1st ed.
    p. cm.—(Essential careers)
Includes bibliographical references and index.
ISBN 978-1-4488-9477-2 (library binding)
1. Landscaping industry—Vocational guidance—Juvenile literature.
2. Landscape gardening—Vocational guidance—Juvenile literature. I.
Title. II. Series: Essential careers.
SB472.5.G47 2013
712.023—dc23

2012040217

Manufactured in the United States of America

CPSIA Compliance Information: Batch #S13YA: For further information, contact Rosen Publishing, New York, New York, at
1-800-237-9932.

contents

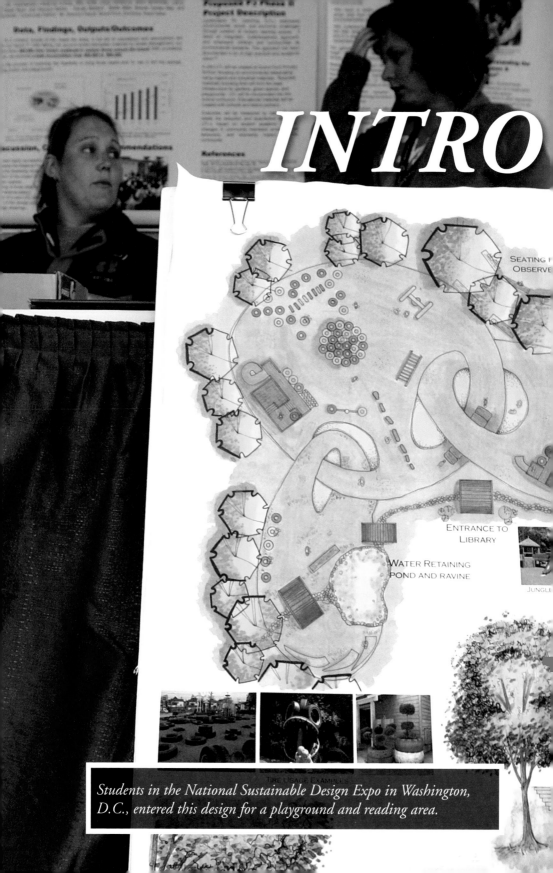

INTRO

Students in the National Sustainable Design Expo in Washington, D.C., entered this design for a playground and reading area.

DUCTION

Landscaping and gardening are great careers for people who like to work outdoors. They're also great careers for people who like to work in air-conditioned offices. They're for daydreamers with colorful imaginations, as well as folks who enjoy doing the same physical tasks over and over every day. Many people may not be sure what kind of landscaping or gardening work they want to do, but most are probably certain of one thing: they want to get paid for doing it.

Any child who has built a town in a sandbox or a castle on a beach knows something about landscaping. Some of those kids later become designers or architects. They're still having fun creating cool spaces, only now as adults, they're doing it for real and they're getting paid for it. Most people start to appreciate gardening sometime after sandbox age. That's probably because plants grow on their own schedules, and it takes time to see the results of a gardener's work. But if you've ever watered a flower or pushed a mower, you have some potentially valuable know-how. If you like the idea of working with earth and plants—and doing good things for the natural environment—read on. There are more kinds of jobs out there than most people realize, and new ones are being created all the time.

The entry-level, or starting, jobs for most people in landscaping and gardening often include the same kinds of work: digging, raking, composting, weeding, watering, mowing, trimming, loading stuff, and hauling it somewhere and unloading it somewhere else. Many of these jobs require muscle or workers who want to build muscle. Lawn care is probably the most common entry-level job, and it's a good place to start for several reasons.

It doesn't have to be a stopping place, though. Just about everyone has special talents, passions, and skills: a gift for writing, drawing, computers, dealing with people, public speaking, or media can guarantee that a career doesn't get boring or monotonous.

Landscapers are mostly concerned with the places where plants grow and how the land is used. Gardeners pay most of their attention to the plants themselves. Some of these jobs are the same as they have been for thousands of years, and some are new, made possible by computers and other scientific advances. It's a pretty safe bet that there will be plenty of jobs in these fields for years to come. The baby boom generation is one reason for this. In the years following World War II (1939–1945), many more babies were born than at any time in U.S. history. Those boomers now make up the bulk of homeowners in America. They know that attractive lawns and gardens make their homes more valuable. That's just one reason why the demand for landscaping and lawn care professionals is as strong as it's ever been, and it's likely to stay that way.

chapter 1

WHAT LANDSCAPERS DO

Landscapers plan and carry out projects in all kinds of places, wherever people need space to be or just space to look at. Besides private lawns and gardens, they work on school grounds and shopping malls, parks, playgrounds, sports fields, golf courses, cemeteries, highways, theme parks, hotels, and many other places. A landscape architect or designer may plan the location of walkways, trees, grass, shrubs, flowers, and just about everything else you'll see in a given area. Landscape workers put those elements in place.

Some landscaping jobs don't require much school education, but all jobs require some work education. Entry-level landscapers often start their careers in the same place as people who go into gardening: on the lawn. Some people find grass mowing, trimming, weeding, and other yard work too hard or too boring to consider, especially if they have to do those chores at home without getting paid. It's amazing how a salary makes work a little less hard and boring.

Many people don't mind yard work, however, and some totally enjoy it. After all, you're basically on your own, you're outdoors, there's often sunshine, and things can be pretty peaceful after the mower is shut down. Some daydreamers might come up with more efficient ways to do the job; they might see how different plants or trees would give more shade, more color, or something good to eat. They might see a path

A forester, at center, advises Missouri high school students on planting an eastern white pine tree to make a windbreak.

where there was no path before. A professional landscaper might see the same things.

LEARNING ON THE JOB

Getting experience with yard work can pay off later on. For example, you quickly learn how long it takes to do the work on a certain-sized area. That information will come in handy if you're ever planning your own project or supervising a work crew. There's nothing like mowing, watering, and weeding to show you how well a space has been designed—or how poorly. Gardeners are usually the first to spot problems. People planning a career in landscaping or gardening can think of yard work as an education without school. By paying attention, it's possible to learn what works and what doesn't, right at ground level.

Landscape workers shovel dirt and push wheelbarrows, and they often do a lot of sweating. The work is almost always outdoors, often in the hot sun or chilly wind. Some laborers move up from those chores to become boss of a work crew, or the supervisor of several crews, on jobs that may be miles apart. A landscape construction foreman might spend a lot of time driving from job to job and

Workers lay concrete in a residential garden. The practice of using concrete, tiles, rocks, and other hard materials in landscapes is called hardscaping.

might also work part of the time in an office. Duties may include hiring and firing, dealing with clients at the job site, finding a replacement when someone is sick, and making sure the workers have the tools and supplies they need.

Laborers in landscape construction and maintenance are often paid by the hour, while foremen, supervisors, and landscape managers may get weekly or monthly salaries. Supervisors generally make more money than laborers do, but they often have to spend more time on the job. When hourly workers put in more time, they get more pay. Salaried workers usually get the same size paycheck no matter how long they work.

Landscape architects and designers spend a lot of their workdays indoors. Architects— the kind who don't have "landscape" in their job title— design buildings and the indoor elements that make them work. Landscape architects and designers concentrate on the grounds outside and around the buildings. Landscape offices tend to be cool in more ways than one. They often have big windows or skylights to let in natural

Making detailed sketches and plans is an important part of landscape architecture and design work.

sunlight. They traditionally have drafting tables, which are big adjustable squares where they draw plans and sketches. They're often air-conditioned, for the computers as well as their comfort's sake. Design software is an important tool.

PICTURE THIS

Architects and designers love pictures—of their work and others', and their Web sites often let you peek into their offices. You can get an international feel for the profession by browsing design studio sites around the world in just a few minutes. The American Society of Landscape Architects (http://www.asla.org) is a good place to start.

Landscape architects are among the highest-paid professionals in the business. The pay figures vary from year to year, but the U.S. Bureau of Labor Statistics keeps the most recent median pay for landscape architects and other jobs at http://www.bls.gov. Landscape architects must be licensed, and they need a bachelor's degree. Landscape design is a similar profession, but it doesn't require a license or a degree.

Designers and architects think not only about the spaces they design but also about the people who use them. They often work directly with clients to get a good understanding of what needs to be done. Their clients may be individuals, companies, schools, or governments. Typical projects for landscape architects include parks, golf courses, sports fields, shopping malls, highways, and campuses.

Many landscapers—both those who plan and those who build—run their own companies. They may work by themselves or hire staff to take on more jobs or bigger ones. Some of the best-educated landscapers naturally work in education. Colleges and universities around the world teach landscape architecture and design, and they're always on the lookout for talented experts to be instructors.

Many landscapers and designers are employees of city, county, state, or federal governments. Some of these government jobs involve drawing up designs, but many involve creating master plans for communities. Local planning departments hire designers who consider not only individual projects but also how those projects fit together. Planners study where to put roads, sewer lines, power lines, and phone lines. They try to make sure the whole system is good for the economy, public health, the environment, and the overall quality of life of the people who live there. They may review environmental impact statements and financial impact statements. These are formal documents that must be approved before big projects

Landscape workers lay mulch at the base of trees in Millennium Park in Chicago, Illinois. City governments provide many of the jobs in the landscaping industry.

can start. People skills are an important asset for planners because they often have to work with political leaders, companies, and citizens who have very different ideas about what's good for the community. Sometimes planners have to be diplomats as well as design experts.

SPECIAL FOCUS

Many architects, designers, and builders have special interests where they focus their work. Some concentrate on environmental restoration—bringing damaged land back to health—or preservation of historical sites such as national monuments and battlefields. Some like to work with certain geographical features: lakes, rivers, seashores, deserts, mountains, grasslands, and gritty inner cities, to list just a few. Some

FROM THE NFL TO LANDSCAPE ARCHITECTURE

Landscape architects have received awards for all kinds of achievements, but only one of them has a Heisman Trophy. Eddie George won college football's top award after an outstanding career at Ohio State University, where he studied landscape architecture. He went on to stardom as a running back in the National Football League (NFL). After retiring from football, he founded George Enterprises and related companies, including EDGE, a planning and design firm.

"We do everything outside the walls of a building, and we try to bring a balance between the two…It's the ability to see the project that starts from scratch, and that piece of paper coming to life," George says in a video produced by the American Society of Landscape Architects.

George says teammates used to kid him about his passion for landscaping. They pictured him laying sod and doing other construction chores, and they didn't understand the creative side of the job. Course work in college got tough at times, and George was tempted to switch majors. But he loved design, and he had a mentor who encouraged him to stick with it. Now George is the one giving encouragement to young people:

"I've gotten plenty of letters from kids who said, 'I didn't know that you were a landscape architect!' or 'I didn't know you studied that! I'm interested in the profession, along with football. How did you do it?

"At the EDGE group, that's our focus: We have fun, we have passion, we're a team, and we enjoy coming up with creative solutions for our environment." Interviews with George are posted on YouTube and Vimeo. His company's Web site is http://www.eddiegeorge.com.

designers specialize in using plants native to their areas.

Therapeutic gardens are becoming more and more popular. These "healing gardens" are places where people can go to relieve stress and recover from injury or illness. On these projects, architects might find themselves working with doctors, psychologists, or yoga instructors. Some of the most entertaining jobs are exactly where you would expect to find them: in the entertainment industry. Theme parks and amusement parks employ thousands of landscape workers and designers, who are constantly updating and taking care of the grounds. For many visitors to Disneyland and other parks, the landscaped floral arrangements are the main attraction.

Landscapers, of course, can't carry out all those tasks without some help. There are many job opportunities in the army of businesses that support landscaping. Many of these jobs are highly specialized. These include irrigation

A team of high school students in Florida created this healing garden, which won scholarship prizes in a competition among teams from the United States and Canada.

experts and soil specialists, who may work for governments and corporations or freelance as independent consultants. Controlling pests—insects and diseases that can threaten plant and human health—is an important specialty. Pest control experts must usually be certified on safe ways to kill bugs without poisoning the environment or making people sick.

Commercial suppliers also hire salespeople with landscape expertise. These companies sell tools and supplies such as pesticides, fertilizers, seeds, plantings, cement, sand, and gravel to landscapers. They need representatives who understand the business and who have contacts among landscapers. Many suppliers have been landscapers or gardeners themselves.

chapter 2

KEEPING IT GREEN

When people picture gardeners, they often think of maintenance gardeners, who work just about everywhere, especially in the summertime. Maintenance gardeners mow and trim lawns; they weed and clean parks and roadsides. Depending on the size of the job, they may need to sow seed, spread mulch, or fix an irrigation system. Maintenance gardeners work for small homeowners and grand estates, cities, counties, states and the federal government, and big companies and small ones.

There are many different kinds of maintenance gardening jobs and several different ways of getting paid for them. Most of the starting jobs involve manual labor, and the work is outdoors, in most kinds of weather. The majority of these jobs also require some muscle. That doesn't mean you need to be a bodybuilder, but you'll probably need to be able to lift, push, pull, and carry loads.

Maintenance gardening is a common job for people who start working as soon as they finish high school. Sometimes it may seem like the only place to start. That's not necessarily bad. Anybody who has mowed a lawn has experience as a maintenance gardener. Anyone who has a lawn is a potential employer. Many people do it all their lives.

For others, maintenance gardening is a stepping-stone to something else in the field. They may decide to start their own

Is this tree healthy? A landscape gardener checks the trunk of a beech tree before planting.

landscaping or gardening company, or they might look for a steady payroll job with company benefits. Eventually, they'll get promoted to crew chief or foreman, or they may decide to go to college for a horticulture degree. Wherever you go, basic ground-level gardening is good experience, and many careers are impossible without it.

How Work Works

Maintenance gardeners sometimes work on their own, sometimes in crews of two to four. They may arrive in a pickup truck full of mowers, blowers, and other equipment, taking care of several lawns in one neighborhood before moving on to work somewhere else. This might be steady work. Some crews maintain the same neighborhoods, doing the same job every week at a certain time, getting regular monthly payments and (hopefully) holiday bonuses from the same customers year after year.

Many gardeners are full-time employees of companies or schools, taking care of the grounds where they work. These are employees on a company payroll, and they may be entitled to company-wide benefits such as health insurance and retirement plans. They may work at apartment complexes, school campuses, corporate buildings, government buildings, zoos, theme parks, city parks and recreation areas, hospitals, army bases, sports fields, or malls. For pay and other national statistics on grounds maintenance work, see http://www.bls.gov/ooh/Building-and-Grounds-Cleaning/Grounds-maintenance-workers.htm.

Another typical arrangement is for gardeners to be employed by a maintenance company as full-time or part-time workers. Gardening and landscaping maintenance companies are often known simply as "contractors" because they make contracts, or agreements, with property owners to take care of their grounds. The property owners pay the contractor, and the contractor pays the worker. Some contractors keep their workers on a payroll as regular employees, who can plan on working every day. Other companies may not have long-term contracts with their clients or a regular payroll. With these

A gardener in Colonial Williamsburg, Virginia, places tree branches to support a crop of peas as they grow. Many gardeners and landscapers specialize in taking care of historic sites.

companies, there's no guarantee that everyone who shows up for work will be sent on a job.

Thousands of maintenance gardeners work as day laborers, getting paid by the hour or by the single job. It's a way to earn money and get experience—and a way to earn more important things: the respect of bosses and coworkers, as well as a reputation for doing good work. When a lot of people are looking for just a few jobs, your reputation is your advertising campaign.

However, day labor has some serious drawbacks in the financial department. For one thing, there's no job security—just because you make good bucks today doesn't always mean there will be work tomorrow. One-time-only jobs often mean working in a different place every day or so, for different people you just met. Even when the pay is good and the jobs go smoothly, it's hard to build a reputation for doing good work because all your employers may be strangers, to you and to one another.

One way around that problem is references. When an employer likes your work, don't be afraid to ask: "Would you mind if I used you as a reference for my next job?" Keep a list of names and numbers of employers who will recommend you. It might come in handy when you apply for full-time work. Besides, you never know when the next boss might ask for a reference. Business cards may be old-fashioned, but they're cheap or free, and they're often the best way to help employers reach you. Cards with pictures work best. They help employers recognize and remember you.

NURSERIES AND A RICH UNCLE

Most plants growing in gardens, lawns, and landscapes start their lives in nurseries and greenhouses. Many jobs start there, too. Commercial nurseries are places where seeds are germinated and seedlings are nurtured until the plants are big enough to sell. Nurseries grow trees and shrubs, flowers and vegetables, grasses and succulents, ferns and cacti. They sell their plants to retail shops, landscapers, commercial gardeners, and home gardeners. Most nurseries are small businesses. Of the thousands of nurseries in the United States and Canada, only a few have more than twenty employees. Most have fewer than four workers. Nurseries and greenhouses are usually local operations, and most welcome job applications from local people. Garden centers are the retail branch of the gardening industry. Many are local outlets of big national companies, but these stores are also usually run by neighborhood people. Garden centers can be good places to look for apprenticeships and jobs, especially in the summer when things get busy. Some larger companies have nurseries and retail stores combined in their garden centers.

In the family of landscaping and gardening jobs, golf is the rich uncle. Golfers spend millions of dollars a year to

This nursery in Florida is a multimillion-dollar business. It ships young bromeliads to flower growers around the world.

play, and golf courses spend millions on construction and maintenance. Companies make millions selling seed, turf, fertilizers, pesticides, and irrigation equipment. For greens-keepers, groundskeepers, supervisors, and course workers, salaries are usually higher than average.

Golf courses and sports fields often have other advantages for people who work there—besides the obvious benefits for sports fans. Home lawns and other landscaped

Grounds crew workers mow fairways during the 2007 U.S. Open at Oakmont Country Club in Pennsylvania. Turf management calls for special know-how, but it offers lots of steady jobs.

spaces are left under snow for much of the year in many parts of the country. Golf courses and sports fields need at least some care all year round. The general rule is that the growing season in the United States—the peak season for gardeners—gets longer the farther south you go.

Turf specialists need more technical know-how than the average home lawn worker. They often have to work with big irrigation systems and heavy equipment. It's important for turf managers to know the proper uses and dangers of fertilizers and pesticides because the areas they care for are so big. That means there may be a greater chance of rain or irrigation runoff carrying poison into nearby water supplies. Many local and state governments require certificates of training for anyone who uses these materials.

Irrigation itself is a big issue for golf courses. They're often criticized for using so much water at a time when water supplies are running low in many areas, and the cost of water is rising. Some courses and governments require special training for repair and maintenance work on irrigation systems.

ALL TALENTS WELCOME

You don't have to work in a garden to have a successful career in gardening. There's always entertainment!

Landscaping and gardening are prime material for television and radio producers, media personalities, writers, and Web site designers. The Web is loaded with blogs on gardening. Sites offer tips on growing just about every species of plant you can imagine, and television channels such as HGTV specialize in landscaping and gardening shows.

Somebody has to think of ideas for the episodes, write the scripts, find people to talk to, and decide where to point the camera, and they can all expect to be paid for their work.

Communication skills—writing, reading, and speaking—are just as important in these lines of work as gardening skills. Most people have more types of talent than they realize; when they recognize all of their talent, interesting things can happen.

Tim Womick grew up loving trees, but he didn't set out to become an arborist. He studied acting, theater design, and production at North Carolina School of the Arts. Today, Womick is known as an "environmental performer." He travels the country, using jokes and music to entertain live audiences at schools and fairs. He also appears on TV and radio shows and Web videos. One of his inspirations is Johnny Appleseed, the legendary pioneer who traveled across America planting trees just because he loved trees.

Womick's act is all about trees: planting them, caring for them, climbing them, and enjoying them. In 2011, he received the True Professional award from the International Society of Arboriculture.

DON'T LOOK DOWN!

Arborists are experts on trees, especially trees growing in cities and towns. Once known as "tree surgeons," arborists usually work with individual trees or small groups of them. People who care for entire forests work in the separate field of forestry.

Trees have a hard time in cities because of pollution and other stresses. Often their root systems are covered up by concrete. However, trees are important to the health of cities because they provide shade, filter dust, and release oxygen into the air. They also serve as windbreaks, screen ugly views, allow some privacy, and mark property lines. Arborists not only plant and transplant trees, they also prune away branches that may be unsafe or that interfere with traffic and power lines. They know how to treat tree diseases and insect pests.

Arborists work in a giant coast redwood tree in California. Tree care specialists need to be physically fit, and their job is not one for people who are afraid of heights.

Climbing is often part of an arborist's job, especially when it's time to prune limbs. This activity requires physical fitness, and those who are afraid of heights need not apply. Trainees usually start as assistants working on the ground. They may load and unload equipment or operate a wood chipper, chopping trimmed-off branches into mulch. Tree work can be dangerous and demanding. Besides the risk of falling, there's often a need to work in winter, when trees may be damaged by ice storms or heavy snow.

Some of the best places to combine work and education are botanical gardens and arboreta. These are places where trees and other plants are cultivated for display, research, and education. (Arboreta are traditionally tree gardens, while botanical gardens feature all kinds of plants.) Botanical gardens and arboreta are often owned by communities, universities, or foundations. There are hundreds of them in the United States and abroad. Many botanical gardens and arboreta offer public programs and classes in gardening, as well as tours and lectures. Many also serve as research laboratories. They need workers who know how to do skilled maintenance gardening and employees who can help with all their other activities.

chapter 3

LEARNING ABOUT LANDSCAPING

Some people make careers in landscaping after studying for years in high school and college. Others start working full-time as soon as they're old enough, getting real experience and real paychecks. Each path has its advantages and disadvantages, but there are a few facts that hold true for both. They're pretty obvious:

- People who do good work tend to get good jobs.
- You can't do good work until you've learned how.
- Employers want to know what you've done and what you've learned.

There are lots of ways to learn about landscaping, inside and outside of school. Let's look at some school courses, activities, and work-study opportunities for students who might want to work in landscaping, whether they intend to go to college or not.

WHY WAIT?

Lots of people become interested in landscape architecture because they like to draw, and high school art classes are probably a good idea for anybody who wants to keep studying in the field. Math, science, geography, computer science,

A botany class takes a field trip in Utah. Botanists study all kinds of plants, whether or not they're useful in gardening.

and English are other helpful courses. If you're considering starting your own business, then business courses are a must.

If you have some colleges in mind, check to see if they have prerequisites—high school courses that you have to pass before you can be admitted. Seniors may also check to see whether their favorite school has visiting days for prospective students. Most colleges do. High school seniors can get campus tours, talk with professors and students majoring in landscape architecture, find out about scholarships, and check out the living arrangements. Colleges and universities try to attract the top students, and admission can be competitive. Good high school grades are obviously critical.

School activities such as science fairs and service clubs such as 4-H are other great places to learn about landscaping and gardening, pick up practical experience, and showcase any work

Workers get ready for Valentine's Day at a flower shop in Chicago. The holiday is one of the busiest times of year for florists.

you've done. The Boy Scouts award a merit badge for landscape design.

Want to work in an architecture firm? Why not ask? Find a list of local companies on the Web, and check their sites or e-mail to see if they have internships for high school students. The American Society of Landscape Architects (http://www.asla.org) has members all over the country. A school counselor might have contacts and suggestions for the best places to try. A librarian can certainly steer you to reference lists of companies, organizations, and individuals who do the work you're interested in. Internship pay is likely to be little or nothing, but the experience can be invaluable. Ask early. Don't wait until it's almost summer.

Other places to look for internships, part-time work, and summer work include golf courses, garden centers, botanical gardens and arboreta, and flower shops. There are many more, and with luck you can find one that fits your main interests. Whether or not you get paid, learning about landscaping has never been easier. The ideas and the work of architects and designers are all around and free to see, in real life and on the Web.

COLLEGE OR NOT?

To go to college or not? That's a big decision for most students and their families. Traditional college education in the United States means a bachelor's degree, which usually takes four years—maybe five for a landscape architecture degree. Four years at a college or university costs thousands of dollars, and costs are going up all the time. For many teens and their families, that expense might seem like an impossible mountain to climb.

One of the great things about the landscaping field, however, is that nobody has to climb the mountain all in one go. Many successful landscapers start their careers by taking the first reasonable job they can. When they get enough time and money, they might enroll in one or two classes at a time, usually on nights or weekends. By the time they earn a certificate or a degree, they have both work experience and a diploma. That combination makes them very attractive to employers.

Unlike architects, landscape designers don't have to get a degree or pass an exam to

Students in a landscaping class finish a walkway. The students go to Maryland's Frederick County Career and Technology Center, which has classes for people who don't plan to go to college.

get a license. In most places, they can simply go into business. Designers usually work on smaller projects, and they usually don't make as much money as landscape architects. Unless designers can show they have enough training to know what they're doing, they may have a hard time finding work.

Many community colleges and technical schools offer associate's degrees for landscape designers. These usually take two years of study. Typical first-year courses include drafting,

KEEPING TRACK
OF THE FIELD

Landscaping salaries and wages vary from place to place and from year to year. States, provinces, cities, and other governments post a lot of helpful information online about jobs in their regions, and the Bureau of Labor Statistics keeps its *Occupational Outlook Handbook* for all kinds of professions updated on line at http://www.bls.gov/ooh.

Check out the Landscape Architects page as an example. You'll find facts like the median pay for the most recent year, the level of education that's required for an entry-level job, how many landscape architects there are in the United States, and if the profession is growing or shrinking. There are also sections on what landscape architects do, where they work, and how to become one.

The American Society of Landscape Architects has all kinds of facts, articles, a list of colleges, and lots of pictures on its site. The Council of Landscape Architectural Registration Boards (CLARB) is an important organization for anybody who wants to work in the field. Every state requires landscape architects to be licensed. CLARB gives the license exam and makes sure applicants have the required education. Its Web site is http://www.clarb.org.

English composition, design principles, algebra, botany, and Spanish. Later courses might cover subjects such as site planning, surveying, seasonal plants, specialty plants and gardens, environmental studies, and pest control. Landscape contractors, public parks departments, and other potential employers want their applicants to have an associate's degree at least.

CREDITS, EXAMS, AND CERTIFICATES

Professional certificates are another kind of credential. They show potential clients and bosses that a designer's work is up to national standards. Landscape designers may be certified by the Association of Professional Landscape Designers (APLD; http://www.apld.org). Candidates don't have to have any kind of degree, but they must have four years of experience working in the profession. They must also show the APLD pictures and details of three projects they've completed.

To become a landscape architect, you need at least a bachelor's degree from an accredited college. This degree usually takes four to five years to complete. You must also pass the Landscape Architect Registration Examination, or LARE. Every state has its own licensing rules, but all states require candidates to pass the test. Students who major in landscape architecture take a mix of arts and science courses. These may include anything from literature and art history to earth sciences and horticulture. Civil engineering, construction law and contracts, design and color theory, drafting, management, meteorology, structural design, surveying, and planning are also on most course lists.

The licensing exam is given on computers by the Council of Landscape Architectural Registration Boards (CLARB). It's divided into four sections. Each section is 80 to 120 questions

Seattle, Washington, landscape architect Michelle Arab is also an artist. She gathered these tule reeds for a sculpture.

long. Many of them are multiple-choice (one right answer) or multiple-response (several possible right answers). Applicants may spend two to four hours on each section. It sounds daunting, but the CLARB also helps candidates prepare by providing detailed instructions and sample questions. To see what the exam looks like, check http://www.clarb.org/Candidates/Pages/PreparefortheExam.aspx.

Because a landscape designer doesn't need a degree at all, why are the requirements so tough for architects? It's true that the work of architects and designers is often similar, but landscape architects can work on larger projects that involve complex technical know-how. These projects may include big infrastructure systems: things like irrigation, lighting, streets, or paths. Designers usually work on gardens, lawns, and other smaller, simpler jobs.

A master's degree can take up to three years or longer to complete, depending on the candidate's undergraduate degree. Students with a degree in landscape architecture may take only a year or two. They typically focus on an area of special interest and write a thesis. Students with a degree in something besides landscape architecture can also enter most master's degree programs, but it takes longer to complete the work, usually three years. All advanced college work usually involves hands-on work in design studios and workshops as well as theory courses. Most colleges hook students up with mentors, professional advisers, and internships, and they do their best to help their graduates find jobs.

THE MOST IMPORTANT LESSONS

There are some things everyone needs to know, whether they're looking for their first job or already have one. Most regular jobs have written safety rules, but it's common sense to take responsibility for your own health on the job. That means learning the hazards of the trade, how to avoid them, and how to keep from hurting yourself and other people. Injury can be a sudden and painful way to end a career, or even a life.

Landscaping and gardening tools have all kinds of blades and edges, and they're often moving very fast. Emergency rooms treat tens of thousands of people each year for lawn mower injuries alone. Many of these injuries are mangled fingers and hands, but most mower injuries are actually caused by rocks and other objects that get hit by the blades and go flying in any direction. Trimmers and blowers kick up millions of tiny eye hazards, and the noise on some jobs can be deafening. More advanced tools bring more advanced risks. Workers under the age of eighteen aren't supposed to use hoists and cranes such as cherry pickers or high-power blade tools such as wood chippers. Eighteen is the minimum age for driving a motor vehicle on the job, although federal rules say seventeen-year-olds may drive in certain situations. Vehicle accidents are a major cause of injury in the landscaping industry for several reasons. Because many jobs are far apart, workers have to spend extra time on the road. In addition, many work vehicles are oversized or undersized. They may have trailers, racks, hoists, or lifts that also need to be operated. If you can drive a car, how tricky can it be to drive a work truck? It's trickier than you might think if you haven't been trained on the work truck.

Tools are just one of many potential job hazards. How much do you know about sunstroke, frostbite, poisonous snakes, poisonous spiders, scorpions, poison ivy, poison oak, and poison sumac? How about poisonous chemicals, which include gasoline? Many job sites are also crisscrossed with high-voltage electrical lines, and electrocution is a danger.

Careful, it's sharp! Blades and machinery are major causes of accidents among gardeners. Safety training is essential.

Goggles, earplugs, hard hats, gloves, safety boots, breath filters—these are all tools of the trade, but they're often not enough to protect people from their own mistakes. Most regular employers are required by law to provide the safety equipment necessary for the job, and they're forbidden to order employees to do hazardous work without the proper training. Some bosses do, however. Employers who hire day laborers for small jobs usually don't provide anything but pay. Whether it's strictly legal or not, workers in those jobs have to look out for themselves, so it pays to know how. Each state has its own job safety regulations, and so does the federal government. The U.S. Occupational Safety and Health Administration (http://www.osha.gov/youngworkers/workers.html) explains workers' and employers' rights and responsibilities, and it has lots of other safety advice.

chapter 4

LEARNING ABOUT HORTICULTURE

Not all education is school education. Some of the best training comes from listening to bosses and coworkers and from watching how others do it. The important thing is to pay attention, ask questions when things aren't clear, and remember the lessons for next time. It may not sound scientific, but it can be.

Gardening is based on the science of horticulture, which is the study and cultivation of plants and the ways that people can use them. It's known as an "applied" science, which makes it different from botany, a "pure" science. Botanists study plants for their own sake, whether the plants are useful to anybody or not. Whether you're working in school or on the job or both, you're learning how to apply the science of horticulture.

DO I NEED A DEGREE?

There are countless places to learn, and there are many jobs in horticulture and gardening that don't require a college degree. When it comes to figuring out how much education you need for a certain job, there's often no simple, single answer. Many entry-level jobs don't require a degree, but it may be hard to get a promotion without one. In horticultural jobs, it's pretty common to see interns working side by side with highly educated experts on the same tasks.

Many horticulturists like to concentrate on certain types of plants. This moth orchid has just been repotted in moss.

Floriculture is an example of a field with a wide variety of school requirements. Floriculturists specialize in cut flowers and potted plants. Most flower shops don't require a college degree when they're hiring salesclerks. They're probably more concerned about how reliable and honest you are and how well you work with customers. Other floriculturists may do large-scale marketing of floral supplies and products. For these positions, you might need a two-year associate's degree in horticulture or a four-year bachelor's degree with some emphasis in sales and marketing. Other flower specialists may be teachers

These botany students in Florida learn tree climbing and other skills in an ecology program.

or researchers. These jobs absolutely require a degree, probably an advanced degree such as a master's or a Ph.D.

The Cooperative Extension Service at the University of Kentucky publishes a simple, wide-ranging list of horticulture careers, along with the usual educational requirements for each. See http://www.uky.edu/Ag/NewCrops/intro sheets/hortcareers.pdf.

Most colleges offer bachelor's degrees in horticulture, as well as two-year associate's degrees, and there are many certificate study programs. These associate and certificate programs can be a great fit for people who are planning to start a company of their own or work in the family business. They often emphasize business management and administration—vital skills for people who want to run their own companies—and classes are often scheduled on nights and weekends.

EXTENDING A HAND

Cooperative extension programs help small business owners, gardeners, farmers, students, and others with information and expert advice. The Cooperative Extension Service is a branch of the U.S. Department of Agriculture. It has offices at a major college in each state and smaller offices throughout many states. Numerous states have special services for students, including 4-H clubs.

Experts from state colleges give advice and help with things like plant science, conservation, pest control, and soil testing. They also help small businesses and growers find new ways to market their products and new sources of income. Congress established the service in 1914. Today, it reaches more people than ever on the Web (http://www.extension.org).

EXTRACURRICULAR ACTIVITIES

High school courses such as biology, chemistry, and math can be a good introduction to the study of horticulture. Many high schools have gardens where students can get hands-on experience working with plants and soil. Career advisers say it's also a very good idea to get involved in career activities outside school. Garden clubs, 4-H clubs, FFA (Future Farmers of America), and other local organizations are also great places to learn. Those activities also look good on a résumé, whether you're applying for a job or for college.

Future Farmers of America is one of many organizations in which students can learn about gardening and get experience that can lead to better jobs. These FFA members were visiting the parks and monuments in Washington, D.C.

You do have a résumé, don't you? A résumé is a summary of your skills, training, and experience. It's usually a single printed page that an employer reads in order to see how well you're qualified for a job. It usually includes the applicant's name and address, contact information, objective (what kind of job he or she wants), education, accomplishments such as awards and volunteer work, special skills, and sometimes references. There are dozens of Web sites with free sample résumés, and some of them are written for jobs in landscaping and gardening. Search "sample résumé" with your job title to see if there's one for your field.

The nearest botanical garden or arboretum could be an ideal place to work as an intern. Many botanical gardens and arboreta are known for their strong internship programs. Some also feature children's gardens, places where little kids and their families can garden together. This kind of youth gardening became a trend in recent years, and it has been picking up steam across the country. It offers some cool opportunities for high school students who like working with younger children as well as with plants. Botanical gardens and arboreta are often affiliated with local colleges, and their internships may count as course credits. The American Public Gardens Association offers internships and has a directory of internships and summer programs. If cash is more important right now than college credit, nurseries and garden centers hire extra workers during the summer growing season.

Volunteer work can be a chance to get experience, help the community, and brighten up a résumé all at once. Student community service programs have been springing up everywhere in recent years. Not all are related to landscaping and gardening, of course, but many are. Student volunteers frequently pitch in to clean up and beautify abandoned lots and neglected spaces. Local businesses may donate seeds, seedlings,

Janis Marks
1202 Fair Street
Anytown, California 93997
Home: (008) 624-9973 Cell: (008) 989-7389
jtmarks80@anet.net

Objective: Mature and reliable high school graduate seeks a sales position in a garden center to get experience in retail marketing and nursery operations for a future career in nursery management.

Education

Jefferson High School
Graduated 2015

GPA 3.62, top 10 percent of class

Experience

Summer 2014, Greenhouse Assistant, Charles Farm Nurseries

Sales and customer service
Assisted with transplants and care of mature plants

School year 2012–2013, Student Greenhouse Manager, Jefferson High
Responsible for maintenance and cleanup
Supervised two assistants

Summer 2012, Operated my own lawn and garden care business
Maintained lawns and flowerbeds at four homes

Other skills

Proficient on both Mac and PC, spreadsheet and Word programs
Spanish

Awards and activities

Jefferson Garden Club President
Judges' special trophy, Tri-State Science Fair
Organizer of Southside Student Cleanup

References available on request

A résumé lists a job applicant's education, experience, and other information in a simple way so it's easy for an employer to read. Free model résumés for all kinds of jobs are available on the Web.

and other supplies for planting. Volunteer work doesn't have to be in the neighborhood. Outfits such as Global Leadership Adventures (http://www.experiencegla.com) arrange community service trips for teens to Africa, Asia, and South America.

Pitching in to restore and protect the environment earns you career credits in more ways than one. Knowing how to conserve water, protect the planet, and clean up pollution is required for just about every degree and professional credential in the landscaping and horticulture industries. It's hard to get a promotion without it. The official mission of the ASLA emphasizes "careful stewardship, wise planning, and artful design of our cultural and natural environments."

NOT FLASHY, JUST BUSY

P. Allen Smith is not what you'd call a flashy guy, but in the world of gardening and landscaping, he's definitely a celebrity.

The award-winning gardener, designer, author, and media personality grew up in Tennessee, where his family has been in the nursery business for four generations. He won a Rotary International scholarship to study garden design and history in England.

"I spent a long time in the growing part of the industry and moved into independent retailing with our own store," he says, "and then from there, from 1993, began to build a media company with the idea of getting the word out about this industry because I love it." A video of the speech is posted on his Web site at http://www.pallensmith.com/support/media-kit/40-igc-videos.

Smith got the word out, all right. He became the host of two public television shows, and another one that runs in commercial syndication, and he hosted regular shows on YouTube. He made guest appearances on NBC's *Today* show and other shows. He wrote a series of books about gardening and cooking. He designed the gardens and grounds for his home and farm in Arkansas.

Smith blogs on his Web site (http://www.pallensmith.com), which also features gardening and cooking tips as well as videos and other resources. He does a local radio show, he's the subject of many magazine and newspaper articles, and he has a long list of national and local awards.

When he speaks in public, however, he often wears jeans and looks like what he is: a friendly neighborhood gardener. "I'm better with compost than computers," he told one audience. But "the world is changing rapidly, and we have to conform to it as an industry."

THERE'S A SOCIETY FOR THAT

Are you interested in a particular plant variety or species? There's probably a national or international society where you can learn more about it and meet other enthusiasts. The American Horticultural Society lists a few of them on its Web site (http://www.ahs.org), and Web searches will turn up many more. There are associations for people who like violets, bamboo, conifers, orchids, roses, bonsai—even rock gardens.

The golf industry is one of the biggest employers for gardeners, landscapers, and other horticultural specialists. Because golf courses are often heavy users of fertilizers, pesticides, and irrigation water, workers often need to be trained and certified. Golf course superintendents usually need to have college degrees in a major such as agronomy, horticulture, or turf grass management. Business courses, language, communication, and public relations can also be helpful. To be certified by the Golf Course Superintendents Association of America (http://www.gcsaa.org), candidates need to be working as a superintendent and have a body of experience. They take a six-hour test that covers the game of golf, turf management, pesticides, finance, environmental questions, and employee management. Many colleges offer special certificates in turf grass management for golf courses.

How about other sports? The Professional Grounds Management Society (http://www.pgms.org) offers two types of certification. To take the test for certified grounds manager, you need at least an associate's degree and work experience. To take the test for certified grounds technician, you need a high school diploma or general equivalency diploma (GED) and two years of experience.

Professional sports field manager certificates are also available from the Professional Lawn Care Association of America (http://www.landcarenetwork.org). This exam covers agronomy, pest management, administration, and

A sports field manager mows the outfield grass at Lamade Stadium in South Williamsport, Pennsylvania, home of the Little League World Series.

specific kinds of sports fields. The Sports Turf Managers Association (http://www.stma.org) also offers a certificate for sports field managers who pass an examination.

Entry-level tree care assistants don't usually need a college degree. The Tree Care Industry Association (http://www.tcia. org) and the International Society of Arboriculture (ISA; http:// www.isa-arbor.com) offer home study courses and books on tree care. The ISA offers certificates as master arborist, certified arborist/utility specialist, certified arborist/municipal specialist, and certified tree worker/climber specialist.

chapter 5

BEING YOUR OWN BOSS

One of the best things about going into business for yourself is that you can start up as soon as you're ready. For most jobs in the United States, the minimum age is fourteen. Even fourteen-year-olds usually need work permits and approval by parents, and their working hours are limited. These rules apply to people who want to be employed by a company or by someone outside their family.

To work in your parent's business, however, there is no age limit. Kids may start their own businesses no matter how old they are. (Those who do are subject to the same rules as every other business owner, including federal, state, and local tax laws.) Starting your own lawn care business is a great way to find out if you have what it takes to be an entrepreneur.

People often think of entrepreneurs as jet-setters worth billions, who never seem to do any real work. A few of them are. But most entrepreneurs aren't rich, and they work constantly. An entrepreneur is simply someone who goes into business for himself or herself, rather than working for somebody else. Most entrepreneurs in the United States are owners of small businesses.

If you like landscaping or gardening work, then running your own show might sound like a great idea. You're the boss! You get to decide when to go to work and when to quit. You can decide whether to take on certain jobs or turn them down. It beats taking orders, doesn't it?

A man lays turf in a garden. People who run their own landscaping and gardening businesses often must know what to do without being told.

Maybe it does, maybe it doesn't. Some people are great at managing their own companies, and others are complete failures. Doing good work—whether it's landscaping, gardening, or designing—is essential, of course. Unfortunately, it's not enough. When businesses fail, it's not usually because they sell bad products or provide bad services. It's because the businesses aren't run properly. They may have problems with customer relations, managing finances, and hiring and firing. Or they may fail to have an overall long-term plan.

WHAT'S YOUR TYPE?

A lot of people are great at their work, but they don't have the personality traits to make them successful business owners. What are those attributes? Counselors and other experts say that successful entrepreneurs usually have most, if not all, of the following characteristics:

- They're disciplined. Everyone has days when they just don't feel like working. Maybe there's something better to do—friends arrive from out of town, or someone suggests a trip to the lake. Maybe it's just a good day to stay in bed. Ideas like that don't mean a thing to clients, who expect work to get done on schedule.

- They're self-starters. They naturally look for the next right thing to do, and they don't have to be told to do it. This kind of motivation is important for keeping a business going when things are slow. For example, many contracting businesses take on snow removal jobs in the winter, when there's not a lot of gardening work to do.
- They have a head for figures. Bookkeeping and bill paying are vital for every business. It's not necessary to be a math expert. An owner can hire an outside specialist to help with payrolls, budgets, and taxes. But successful entrepreneurs always have a good idea of where their money's coming from and where it's going.
- They enjoy dealing with other people. These individuals include customers, employees, and vendors—those who provide equipment and supplies. It helps to be outgoing, to enjoy chatting, and to be able to remember names—not just clients' names, but also those of others you may meet, such as clients' spouses or children. Many successful businesses even keep track of customers' birthdays and anniversaries so that they can send cards or say the right thing at the right time. This sort of thing may seem like phony friendship, but in business, it's basic customer relations.
- They're good at organizing and helping other people get organized. They can keep in mind the big picture, or the most important things. At the same time, they're able to keep track of little details. If there are too many details to remember, they make lists. And they remember where the lists are kept.

COMPOSTS & SOILS

Revitalizer ..... 19 50 ... 31 95
Manure 18 50
Turkey

untry Gard

oil 14

Soil [when available] 11

For successful business owners, getting along well with people may be just as important as being a good landscaper or gardener.

- They're original thinkers. They can imagine new ways to do things and new things to do. They're also open to new possibilities, and they're not afraid to look at new problems.
- They're good at communicating. They can clearly express what needs to be done, and they're able to hear, see, and understand what needs doing. They can do this by talking and listening, as well as by reading and writing.
- They have patience. They know it takes time to build a business and make it profitable. They don't expect things to happen right away. They realize that they must sometimes depend on others, who may work at a slower pace. They're able to keep plugging away at tasks they may not like.

Probably the most important requirement for a successful entrepreneur is a burning desire to succeed. If you're thinking of starting a business just because you don't like working for somebody else, it might be a good idea to think again. There will be complications, setbacks, and a lot of uncertainty before you start to feel comfortable. It can get discouraging. Those without a strong will to win will often give up.

WHAT'S THE PLAN?

Whether you're starting a neighborhood lawn care business now or a full-scale company later on, it's a good idea to start with a plan. In the world of entrepreneurs, writing business plans is a fine art. These plans are often long documents full of detail, and they follow a strict format. Moneylenders study business plans closely before deciding to finance an entrepreneur.

If you're not planning to ask for a loan, a business plan doesn't need to be hundreds of pages long. It should be long enough to answer some important questions, such as:

1. What services will I offer customers?
2. Who are my customers, and how many will there be?
3. How much will I charge?
4. How much will it cost me to do business?
5. Who is my competition?
6. How will I get customers to choose me instead of them?
7. What tools, permits, supplies, and other things do I need to get started?
8. How am I going to pay for those things?
9. How am I going to get to the jobs with my equipment?
10. How am I going to find new customers?

All those questions have thousands of possible answers, of course. The answers are different for every company, and there are thousands of companies. The U.S. Census Bureau counts more than ninety thousand landscaping and lawn care companies. There are more than thirty-eight thousand retail nurseries and lawn and garden supply stores, according to Manta, a small business Web site. Many of those have only one, or just a few, employees. More than one hundred thousand nurseries grow and sell plants and seedlings in the United States, and most of them are also small operations, with four or fewer employees.

Scouting out the territory and planning are also important because the picture is constantly changing for many types of businesses. There are more than one million U.S. flower shops, but thousands of them went out of business following the

A worker in a garden center moves plants in a nursery. Many garden centers grow their own plants as well as sell them to customers.

economic slump in 2008. Traditional shops have also been losing out to online flower sellers.

All these businesses depend on other companies to supply their tools, seeds, fertilizer, fuel, office supplies, and other needs. Many of these suppliers are huge or medium-sized corporations, but some are also smaller entrepreneurial businesses.

BACK TO SCHOOL

When landscaping, gardening, and other small businesses fail, it's usually not because their owners made mistakes in their work. It's because they made mistakes in running their business. One common beginner's mistake is focusing on the job, thinking the business will take care of itself. Poor planning, bad decisions, poor customer relations, competition, and cash problems are just a few of the problems that can cause a business to fail, even if the owner is great with plants, lawn care, or landscape work.

IT TAKES MORE THAN ONE KIND OF TALENT

Being a successful entrepreneur takes more than one kind of talent. Michael Podlesny remembers that he was seven or eight years old when his father introduced him to gardening. He went on to create Mike the Gardener Enterprises in Burlington, New Jersey, selling vegetable, fruit, and herb seeds online. But he didn't stop there.

Podlesny used his Web, software, and marketing skills to promote gardening and his products in all kinds of ways. He made himself available for TV and Web interviews, giving free gardening advice. He made himself an expert on ways to help businesses through social media, like Facebook, Twitter, and Pinterest.

Mike the Gardener's Web site (http://www.averagperson gardening.com) features podcasts, downloads, how-to articles, and videos not only on gardening but also on marketing and promoting your own business. He wrote a book, *Vegetable Gardening for the Average Person*. He came up with the idea for a Seeds of the Month Club, which became his most successful item. He also started a Seeds for Schools program. While he was doing all that, he found time to continue gardening with his kids.

"I have been growing veggies for over thirty years, and it is so exciting to see a tiny seed grow into a large plant that yields fresh produce," he said in a press release announcing his book. "In vegetable gardening, you truly do reap the fruits of your labor."

High school and college business courses—taken in person or on the Web—are an important foundation for anybody who wants to start a business. These courses usually include subjects such as office administration, Web and computer skills, accounting, business law, and finance. Some schools arrange student internships with local businesses—obviously a great way to learn firsthand.

"How do I start my own business?" Type that question into Google and you'll find plenty of books, magazines, blogs, and Web sites offering help for entrepreneurs of all ages. The U.S. Small Business Administration (http://www .sba.gov) is one of the most extensive and reliable sources of help. Nonprofit organizations such as Score (http://www .score.org) connect business newcomers with experienced mentors, hold workshops, and post advice on the Web. Score hosts tools such as templates for business plans and tips such as the "60-Second Guide for Handling Upset Customers." To avoid upsets, clients can also find customer relations advice, including "8 Ways to Make Customers Love a Local Business."

Whether you're planning to work for yourself or for an employer, in a big company or a one-person lawn care business, it's hard to succeed without a professional attitude. Being professional means keeping agreements, showing up on time with the right tools, and putting in a full day's work. That's just for starters. It means learning how to do the job properly, whether you learn at school, at work, or by volunteering. It also means getting paid—and paid well for good work. Quality work means not only more money; it might also lead to a greater choice of jobs. Landscapers and gardeners with a reputation for good work usually have an easier time finding work, no matter what their chosen field.

glossary

accredited Officially recognized as meeting a set of standards.

administration The activity of running an organization or business.

agronomy The science of soil management and crop production.

appreciate To recognize the value of something.

certified Proven or tested to meet certain qualifications.

client Someone who uses the services of a professional, usually for pay.

composting Fertilizing with decayed material such as cuttings, waste food, or manure.

consultant Someone who gives expert professional advice, usually for pay.

creative Able to come up with original ideas; full of imagination.

credential A document that proves someone's qualifications.

diplomat Someone who can deal smoothly and effectively with people.

germinate To sprout or start to grow.

irrigation The act of watering land so that plants can grow on it.

maintenance Keeping something in good condition.

marketing All the things a business must do in order to get its products to the buyer; these include advertising, selling, and shipping.

median The middle value in a set of numbers.

mentor Someone with experience who's trusted to advise another person.

payroll A list of employees who are entitled to regular pay.

preservation The act of keeping something the way it's intended to stay.

profession An area of work that requires specialized knowledge and has a set of standards.

professional Someone who has specialized knowledge of his or her work and a set of standards for doing it.

promotion Putting out information about a product or business in order to increase sales or public awareness.

résumé A written summary of someone's education, work history, and professional accomplishments.

salary A fixed payment for work done, usually paid monthly or every two weeks.

specialized Concentrated on one area.

statistics The collection and analysis of large quantities of numerical data.

technical Requiring special knowledge.

template A model or pattern that others can copy.

theory course A school course that focuses on the principles that make something work.

transplant To take up a growing plant and plant it in another place.

wage Payment to a worker, usually by the hour, day, week, or individual job.

for more information

American Horticultural Society (AHS)
7931 East Boulevard Drive
Alexandria, VA 22308
(703) 768-5700
Web site: http://www.ahs.org
The AHS is one of America's oldest national gardening
associations. It has many internship opportunities and
other programs for young gardeners and designers,
including its National Children and Youth Garden
Symposium.

American Public Gardens Association (APGA)
351 Longwood Road
Kennett Square, PA 19348
(610) 708-3010
Web site: http://www.publicgardens.org
The APGA is an association of botanical gardens, therapeutic
gardens, nature centers, sculpture gardens, arboreta, parks,
college campuses, zoos, cemeteries, and historic landscapes
in the United States and Canada. It publishes information
on jobs and internships.

American Society of Landscape Architects (ASLA)
636 Eye Street NW
Washington, DC 20001-3736
(202) 898-2444 or (888) 999-2752
Web site: http://www.asla.com
The ASLA is the professional association for landscape architects,
with seventeen thousand members. It offers mentor

programs, surveys of top colleges, job information, and other services. Its site has stories and pictures of what a landscape architect does and how to become one.

Canadian Society of Landscape Architects (CSLA)
P.O. Box 13594
Ottawa ON K2K 1X6
Canada
(866) 781-9799
Web site: http://www.csla-aapc.ca
The CSLA is the voice of the landscape architecture profession
   in Canada. Its site has a list of accredited colleges, job
   postings, and information about landscape architecture.

Environment Canada
Inquiry Centre
10 Wellington, 23rd Floor
Gatineau QC K1A 0H3
Canada
(819) 997-2800
Web site: http://www.ec.gc.ca
Environment Canada is a branch of the government that
   protects the nation's natural resources, among other
   responsibilities. It has information on work programs
   and internships related to horticulture and landscaping.

Professional Landcare Network (PLANET)
950 Herndon Parkway, Suite 450
Herndon, VA 20170
(800) 395-2522
Web site: http://www.landcarenetwork.org
PLANET is an international association for lawn care professionals, maintenance contractors, designers, and other

professionals. It tests and certifies managers and technicians, conducts education programs, and offers scholarships.

U.S. Bureau of Labor Statistics (BLS)
Division of Information and Marketing Services
2 Massachusetts Avenue NE, Room 2850
Washington, DC 20212
(202) 691-5200
Web site: http://www.bls.gov
The BLS provides guides to and statistics on careers in various industries, including landscape and gardening.

WEB SITES

Due to the changing nature of Internet links, Rosen Publishing has developed an online list of Web sites related to the subject of this book. This site is updated regularly. Please use this link to access the list:

http://www.rosenlinks.com/ECAR/Land

for further reading

Avent, Tony. *So You Want to Start a Nursery.* Portland, OR: Timber Press, 2003.

Byzcynski, Lynn. *The Flower Farmer: An Organic Grower's Guide to Raising and Selling Cut Flowers, Revised and Expanded.* White River Junction, VT: Chelsea Green Publishing, 2008.

Careers in Focus: Landscaping and Horticulture. New York, NY: Ferguson, 2008.

Cash, Patrick. *Lawn Care Business Guide: The Definitive Guide to Starting and Running Your Own Successful Lawn Care Business.* Trenton, NJ: Patrick Publishing, 2009.

Crandall, Frank H., III. *The Essential Horticultural Business Handbook.* Wood River Junction, RI: Frank H. Crandall III Horticultural Services, 2011.

Davies, Sophie. *Design Grow Sell: A Guide to Starting and Running a Successful Gardening Business from Your Home.* Petersfield, England: Brightword Publishing, 2012.

Dell, Owen E. *How to Start a Home-Based Landscaping Business.* Guilford, CT: Globe Pequot Press, 2010.

Foster, Kelleann. *Becoming a Landscape Architect.* Hoboken, NJ: Wiley, 2010.

Garner, Jerry. *Careers in Horticulture and Botany.* New York, NY: McGraw-Hill, 2006.

Gibson, Trish. *Brenda Colvin a Career in Landscape.* London, England: Frances Lincoln, 2011.

Hartin, Janet. *FabJob Guide to Become a Landscape Company Owner.* Calgary, AB: FabJob, 2009.

Howard, Love Albrecht. *So You Want to Be a Garden Designer.* Portland, OR: Timber Press, 2010.

Ingels, Jack. *Landscaping Principles and Practices.* Independence, KY: Delmar Cengage Learning, 2009.

LaRusic, Joel. *Start & Run a Landscaping Business.* Bellingham, WA: Self-Counsel Press, 2005.

Linsenman, Ciree. *Start Your Own Lawn Care or Landscaping Business.* Irvine, CA: Entrepreneur Press, 2011.

Mozingo, Louise A. *Women in Landscape Architecture: Essays on History and Practice.* Jefferson, NC: McFarland & Company, 2012.

Parks, Barbara, and Jodi Helmer. *The Complete Idiot's Guide to Green Careers.* Royersford, PA: Alpha Publishing, 2009.

Simms, Barbara. *John Brookes Garden and Landscape Designer: The Career and Work of Today's Most Influential Garden and Landscape Designer.* London, England: Conran, 2007.

Wasnak, Lynn. *How to Open & Operate Your Financially Successful Landscaping, Nursery, or Lawn Service Business.* Ocala, FL: Atlantic Publishing Group, 2010.

bibliography

American Society of Consulting Arborists. "Common Terms." Retrieved September 2012 (http://www.asca-consultants .org/conresources/terms.cfm).

American Society of Landscape Architects. "Career Discovery." Retrieved August 2012 (http://asla.org/CareerDiscovery.aspx).

American Society of Landscape Architects. "Eddie George on Careers in Landscape Architecture." Retrieved August 2012 (http://www.youtube.com/watch?v=N6VAI uVVL3k).

Arboretum Johnston Community College. "Landscape Gardening Certificate Requirements." Retrieved August 2012 (http://www.johnstoncc.edu/arboretum/certificate.aspx).

Bureau of Labor Statistics. "Landscape Architects." Occupational Outlook Handbook. Retrieved August 2012 (http://www.bls.gov/ooh/Architecture-and-Engineering/ Landscape-architects.htm).

Camenson, Blythe. *Opportunities in Landscape Architecture, Botanical Gardens and Arboreta.* Chicago, IL: VGM Career Horizons, 1999.

Careers in Focus: Landscaping and Horticulture. New York, NY: Ferguson, 2008.

Careerwatch. "What Is a Horticultural Therapist?" Wordpress.com. Retrieved August 2012 (http:// careerwatch.wordpress.com/2010/03/09/ what-is-a-horticultural-therapist).

Council of Landscape Architectural Registration Boards. "About Licensure." Retrieved August 2012 (https:// www.clarb.org/Candidates/Pages/aboutlicensure.aspx).

Dell, Owen E. *How to Start a Home-Based Landscaping Business.* Guilford, CT: Globe Pequot Press, 2010.

Foster, Kelleann. *Becoming a Landscape Architect.* Hoboken, NJ: Wiley, 2010.

Garner, Jerry. *Careers in Horticulture and Botany.* New York, NY: McGraw-Hill, 2006.

Jenkins, Mary Zuazua. *National Geographic Guide to America's Public Gardens.* Washington, D.C.: National Geographic Society, 1998.

Linsenman, Ciree. *Start Your Own Lawn Care or Landscaping Business.* Irvine, CA: Entrepreneur Press, 2011.

Manta. "United States Retail Nurseries, Lawn and Garden Supply Stores." Manta Media. Retrieved September 2012 (http://www.manta.com/mb_34_B6105_000/retail_nurseries_lawn_and_garden_supply_stores#?tab=charts-emp_pie).

National Gardening Association. *Dictionary of Horticulture.* New York, NY: Viking Press, 1994.

Nelson, D. "What Does a Department of Planning and Infrastructure Do?" WiseGeek. Retrieved August 2010 (http://www.wisegeek.com/what-does-a-department-of-planning-and-infrastructure-do.htm).

Paulson, Edward. *The Complete Idiot's Guide to Starting Your Own Business.* Indianapolis, IN: Alpha Books, 2000.

Pierce, Todd James. "Castle Gardens—Adventures in Landscaping." Disney History Institute, May 15, 2012. Retrieved August 2012 (http://www.disneyhistoryinstitute.com/2012/05/disneyland-year-one-pt-2.html).

Pohmer, Stan. "2011 State of the Industry: It's Not Over Yet." Florists' Review. Retrieved August 2012 (http://www.floristsreview.com/main/january2011/FeatureArticle0111.html).

Royal Horticultural Society. *Planting a Small Garden.* New York, NY: DK Publishing, 2007.

Womick, Chip. "Thanks to the Trees." Our State North Carolina, April 2010. Retrieved September 2012 (http://www.ourstate.com/tim-womick).

index

A

American Horticultural Society, 53
American Public Gardens
    Association, 50
American Society of Landscape
    Architects, 12, 15, 35, 38, 52
arboreta, 30, 35, 50
arborists, 28, 29–30
Association of Professional
    Landscape Designers, 39

B

botanical gardens, 30, 35, 50
business cards, 24
business plans, 62–65

C

cemeteries, 7
certification, 39, 54, 56
children's gardens, 50
commercial suppliers, 18
cooperative extension programs, 48
Cooperative Extension Service, 48
Council of Landscape Architectural
    Registration Boards (CLARB),
    38, 39–41

D

day laborers, 23, 44

E

EDGE, 15
environmental restoration, 14
entertainment industry, landscaping
    and gardening and, 28
extracurricular activities, 49

F

floriculture, 46–48
flower shops, 35, 46, 63–65

G

garden centers, 24–25, 35
gardening, maintenance, explanation
    of, 19–24
gardening and landscaping
    maintenance companies, 21–23
George, Eddie, 15
Global Leadership Adventures, 52
Golf Course Superintendents
    Association of America, 53–54
golf industry/golf courses, 7, 13,
    25–27, 35, 53–54
government jobs, 13–14, 18, 19
greenhouses, 24

H

highways, 7, 13
historic sites, preservation of, 14

ABOUT THE AUTHOR

Larry Gerber got his first paying job mowing neighbors' lawns at age eleven. During high school and college, Gerber worked summers as a day laborer, and he did landscape construction and maintenance. He is a former Associated Press bureau chief and lives in Los Angeles, California.

PHOTO CREDITS

Cover (landscaper) © iStockphoto.com/Daniel Kourey; cover (background), pp. 1, 12, 43 iStockphoto/Thinkstock; p. 4 Alex Wong/Getty Images; pp. 8–9, 14, 24–25, 36–37, 40, 54–55 © AP Images; pp. 10–11 Andy Sotiriou/The Image Bank/Getty Images; pp. 16–17 © Taylor Jones/The Palm Beach Post/ZUMA Press; p. 20 Aaron Haupt/Photo Researchers/Getty Images; pp. 22–23 Newport News Daily Press/McClatchy-Tribune/Getty Images; pp. 26–27 Getty Images; p. 29 Timothy G. Laman/ National Geographic Image Collection/Getty Images; pp. 32–33 Education Images/Universal Images Group/Getty Images; pp. 34–35 Scott Olson/Getty Images; pp. 46, 49 The Washington Post/Getty Images; p. 47 John B. Carnett/Popular Science/Getty Images; pp. 58–59 Christopher Bissell/Taxi/Getty Images; p. 61 Creatas/Thinkstock; pp. 64–65 Yellow Dog Productions/The Image Bank/Getty Images.

Designer: Matt Cauli; Editor: Kathy Kuhtz Campbell;
Photo Researcher: Amy Feinberg